A Perfect Mirror

For Jill

A Perfect Mirror

Sarah Corbett

Best Wishes,
and Thanks,
Sarah Corbett
March 2018.

First published 2018 by
Liverpool University Press
4 Cambridge Street
Liverpool
L69 7ZU

British Library Cataloguing-in-Publication data
A British Library CIP record is available

ISBN 978-1-78694-101-5 softback

Typeset by Carnegie Book Production, Lancaster
Printed and bound in Poland by Booksfactory.co.uk

For Lugh

Toward that great jewel: shown often,
Never given

Sylvia Plath

Contents

The Commute

I am new to this – six am, dark and rain,
the train an illuminated cabinet
for the half-awake, half-out-of-dream –

initiate to the ritual of ear-bud and book,
coffee held like an offering to the tunnel
that consumes us, eyes bruised pods

consulting the oracle of a discarded *Metro*.
Gun-fire, bomb-blast, kick of bullet so far off
we have to reach with our minds for the turn

of the planet, her colours in that black expanse
tilted and blurred like a child's spinning top,
all the people clinging to it; and you, child,

in your sarcophagus of grit and dirt,
the lid just lifted in some wrecked street
of Aleppo, the centerfold, centrifuge of my gaze,

clay white, your face an effigy, the death mask
of a poet, a flour-dusted prophet waving
one free hand to say: here, I am here; I am alive.

How carefully now they must unbury you –
the bulbs of your eyes, the flowers of your lips –
unsealing your mouth's preserved terracotta

to take your first clear breath for days.
How you must have dreamt, in your cave
of rubble, to be the boy king resurrected

into daylight's lapis lazuli, air's fluid metal.
But who am I to write this? In a few minutes
I will step from the train when it pulls into the station,
blink in the sun gracing the platform, my destination.

Warming

Time was, they would air lift food supplies
to hill farms trenched in snow for months.
We've not seen that here for twenty years.
Christmas is warm and wet, viruses spoiling
through the closed-in valleys like gossip.
February, no doubt, will be the same slide
into March, weeks of white-lid skies, least
path a mud slick, weather a little deeper
in your joins. That year, pipes froze so hard
you had to hold a candle to the joints and hope
for the crack, the break, the fissure in the ice,
a two bar fire on your wall a surgeon's mask,
dull, red, ugly but utterly wonderful when the
power returned. The Thames froze and milk
arrived on skis to burst tops on doorsteps
like over-proved bread; across Devon sheep
cocooned like embryos in blue tombs,
the lamb replete and perfect in its birth sac.
Now these supplicant frostings at New Year
are sticking plasters on the black wound
of the earth, an inch of ice-cube snowballs
friable as buck shot. There's blossom
in the lane, birds have begun their relay
of twig and feather, crows tumble catch-me
in the humid air and we've given up on winter
when all of a sudden overnight in Heptonstall
a muffler drops a white sheet over the moor.

Walking Home

We walked home this way every school day
for seven years, across the field, the grass
in summer long and wet wetting hems
and cuffs or pulled seeding in our hands;
along the lane, cow parsley greeting us
like old men. There were nettles to be skirted,
an abundance of red and purple admirals
not seen this last wet decade, skip of wren
from wall nook to nook, rare start of hare
or stoat and by July the one white foxglove.
In winter the path frosted with sugared lace
and you marveled at the iced puddles as if
the intricate carvings were a miracle never
before seen. After dark we walked hand
in hand under constellations – Orion,
Cassiopeia, Little Bear – turning in the sky
as the months turned us towards spring;
the moon we saw through full and quarter,
sometimes rising like a huge white balloon,
sometimes ringed with clouds like bruises.
We walked in rain and snow and sun, talked,
talked about what now I don't remember
only see the movement of your hands, two small
kites pulling on the strings of your thoughts.
You were never lost and only ever once afraid:
when I got drunk at New Year and fell
in the ditch. Home was always there, waiting
at the end of the muddy drop to the road.

Cycling the Island

The day was a cold one, wind
whipping up curds in the bay,
choughs black dots blown
from the cliffs like a veil.

Anoraks ballooned, my husband
pregnant, a precarious seahorse
on the hired bicycle; our son
on the pedals, the orange bars

of his trainers flashing,
his green coat, I recall, the same
buff-olive as the sea. I had
laundry to do, last night's

washing up, a sweep through
the cottage for sand, fragments
of shell. Next year, I thought,
waving them off, a hotel.

Seems so selfish now, careless,
and careless the word I used
when my husband came back
alone in panic, the wind

behind him. So much care,
to bring a child through his first
nine years, to simply lose
sight of him around a bend in the road.

The Garden
after Andrew Marvell

It was a time of laurels,
a fearless time. I broke away
to write – bed in the woods,
on the river a moon of ice.
Nights unsealed and the knot of
sleep slipped, a beat into waking.
> You came and took my hand
> to show me the garden.

We stepped into a maze of hedges,
each leaf a flower then wings
lifting, that would have lifted me.
A border of tulips stood up
like a row of varnished nails
and I was glad of your company.
> You said it would all be gone
> by morning and we should

taste it. Sacs of green sap showed
our faces, multiple and convex
as in a hall of mirrors. Our mouths
kissed and merged, stretched
to grimaces. We had touched it
and it would remember us, an X
> on a roll of used up ribbon
> typed over itself, and again.

A field of forget-me-nots
were stars, deep as blue; we moved
through a see-through radiance
the texture of honeycombs,
honey-scented, like a thought

unvoiced at the back of the throat.
       It was too much, and you reeled
       me in to the shade of a lucent spot

where we abandoned our skins.
How mossy the ground was,
a green bed for entwining;
a spring ran down to a pool
of brightness where water lilies
budded to pink hearts that opened
       and sang with pink tongues;
       we sang with them, wordless

as birds in the boughs above us.
Mouths of silver uttered a lament
from a grove of birch and hazel,
a sympathetic music.
As dark faltered towards first light
we made a meal of herbs and fungi.
       You blew smoke from the fire
       of sacred things, saying them over.

A wood grew above and around us,
ash and elder running the span
of seasons through berry and seed,
naked as grief, then back to green.
In the distance a chestnut eye
and a chestnut thigh winked:
       a young oak pushed out a hip
       and a rowan shifted to woman.

Let's be clear: this was no Eden
but a journey into the mind
and where the mind goes, gliding
beyond the shores of its ocean
finding another beyond it.
You said, this is your vision

       to be kept and told again
       in some way that fits the telling.

Our time was up. Sycamore pods
fuzzed the air, bees were busy
gathering and an apple tree,
heavily laden, hunched and shook.
I caught both fruits that fell
and rubbed them against my leg
       until they were small white suns.
       We ate in the silence, burning.

Swallow Hole

A dry spell. Gorse starring the rocks
above the ghyll. Far down on a shelf
her body, soft, intact. No more than
three days dead. Maybe she climbed,
nimble as a girl. But her black bob,
glossy in death, is white at the temple
where there is a crack, half-healed,
a row of bilberry beads gone dull.
She died slow. Maybe she fell, leaning
too far in – I've almost done it myself –
smelling depth, darkness, distance;
that breath, that call, that pull.
You have to take care, in such places.
We have ropes, lanterns, body-suits.
On her feet are yellow plastic sandals
over ankle socks greening at the rim,
and there – blue indents on her knees
where she must have knelt,
skin off the back of one hand,
two lines on her neck like tribal marks.
Now I see her, head-down, toppling.

Sylvia Plath's House

There you were, all along,
in your house under the hill,
eking out time among stones
where moss fingers a wall

and narcissi come petal-fisted,
snub-nosed from the clay.
Daily you take a cloth
to your knick-knacks and things

on the mantelpiece, the windowsill,
where dust builds and builds,
time itself passing judgment.
There might be visitors, if only you'd

hear them clamouring at your gate
with their letters of introduction,
if only you could hear all
the lamentation. The town in the crook

of the valley, you say, is a myth.
Nightly you watch the moon
roll like a pill on the cloud's tongue,
trees march in step with the earth.

You've tried the wood's mauve heart
and returned it, hollow as panic.
Below you at Lumb water falls
over the slabbed lip into a pool

black as a barrel of tar, tips its load
into the thousand cups and rings,
the goddess stamping her heel in stone.
You put your hand there until it numbs.

It is always almost spring and you are
watching, watching, your face
at the window a mask, the mouths
of the bee-houses struck dumb.

Sixteen Acres

This is the earth, a portion of it –
the boundary of Wicken Hill
and the line of sight over farms,
moorland, a scattering of houses,
the alert wolf of Heptonstall
Church – these sixteen acres
set above the town like a jewel,
a throne of stillness, a green eye.
In spring there will be hares
leaping under foot in the smoky
dawn and sky-falls of lapwings,
their porcelain of broken nests,
the vetch coming, coltsfoot,
starbursts of clover and trefoil
and when the hay is high lacings
of gold spiders; but it is winter,
trees are wiry sculptures,
rooks carved in the branches,
the only things living, it seems,
crows, and the fox at night
getting his dinner, setting
his trail in this year's snow.
The land is tardy now and wet,
the earth spongy with springs
running over millstone grit
a few feet down – you can hear them.
Put your hand where the ground
opens to the blood warmth,
lie and draw the heat as if
your body were a divining rod,
above you the sky a vast lens

and you its aperture, clouds
beasts dispersing across a field
or souls queuing to enter heaven.

The Trap

Enough to snuff the quick/Of her small heat out
— *SP 'Hardcastle Crags'*

August, a woozy, pollinated afternoon,
heat on the hills like a shawl. Black
stones of the village pile up, black
on black, burnt in the air's oven.

Deep in the valley the wood hugs turns
of enfolded land, a seep of dark water
she pulls towards like a blind thing,
the air heavy as sleep where mill ruins

are a green temple. Lost now, the path
peters out to a rabbit-run and a shortcut
becomes a deadfall into a trill of menace,
the first sting, the next and then a host,

sting after sting in her hair, her mouth.
She can only crawl backwards uphill,
a headful of vibrating barrettes
tiny, spent jewels she shakes out,

hands beating the air like a claxon,
heart clapping to disperse the poison.

Praise Song

I write in praise of the junior doctor who, at four am or some time thereabouts, pale, sweating, swaying foot to foot at the tale-end of a double shift, put his fingers into my uterus and swept the last blood-thickened scraps into a metal dish, what was left of the placenta that hours previously held the faulty but still beating heart of the fourteen week fetus that was never going to, was never meant to make it. He did this because I asked him to, begged, pleaded with him to be spared the mask, the plummet, the counting back into the abyss, anesthetic, the D and C procedure that recalled that other time, that other loss, the one I had chosen. He did this because he could, because in the lemon-walled room with the Peter Rabbit curtains at four in the morning there was just me and him and the small break the baby made in the fabric of things as it slipped away. There he was — younger than me, too young maybe to have suffered much personal loss — pale, sweating, swaying foot to foot, dark blond hair, baby-face, hands deft, making this pact I now break; somehow by chance or fate assigned to me that night when he should have been in bed dreaming, his school jumper rolled for a goal post, tendons primed, arms out-stretched, fingers splayed for the ball as it was kicked his way.

View of a Badger on the Heights Road

It looks a clean death, curled as you are
on the verge, almost relaxed, paws folded
over each other, head turned to the side.
Not a trace of earth on you, killed on a night
walk, perhaps, on this treacherous moor road.
I stand and watch a while in case a heartbeat
or breath disturbs the dense clean fur,
clean enough to touch. But you are still.

There's something wrong with this scene:
you lie collapsed softly into the grass
like my dog at rest after a long walk,
a blue plastic glove thrown into the hedge
behind as if you have been killed elsewhere
and placed here, a carelessness, a misdemeanor.

The Meaning of Birds

Three ravens, or in their absence,
        crows, any black bird, signal a death.
These three on the wall, in the snow,
        in the lane – a teenager or widow

they have enfolded as their own.
        Rooks know loneliness and grief,
know it in their purple gowns,
        their raised skin crowns. What of

the one I watched die? Its fellows paced,
        crawed, nursemaids or executioners
I couldn't tell. Before we came here
        I flew over these woods and fields

like a pigeon homing, dreamt also
        of houses back to back in rows,
rain-black streets and cobbled roads,
        of trees an ingrained seam.

Hillside a water-fall, sky a wedge
        of black distance. On the hill a church
with two black eyes guarding
        its underground and earthly charges.

An eagle means war – rare here
        in the West Riding of Yorkshire –
unless you count the Civil War dead
        seen marching down Market Street,

that corner of the woods we'll not now go.
        What of the peregrine on our fence
that autumn, its chick in the fir tree
        at the bottom of the garden?

What of the collared dove the dog
            pulled from a rabbit hole to flap,
flightless with shock across the field,
            what of the kestrel? There, there it is –

wind-skirted redback, windrider,
            fieldcopter dizzying off the line.
The magpie is a question. Each morning
            a question that never gets answered.

The Ghost of a Flea

after William Blake

What is this that comes, tongue out,
bug-eyed, gripping daintily behind
what could be a tail but is a knife,
come with a bleeding bowl, fingers

curved like long-dead nails? What is this
apparition, stars in the wake of his comet?
The corner of the bedroom housed him,
gigantic in a speck of dust, eyes

soft white pods of spider nests
where the million bodies might
any minute come rushing. These days
I name the horror, frame by frame,

but then there was a pit, me clinging
to it, pushing back at what I could
not see. What is it the poet sees,
now speaking silently, now creeping

from gold curtains, tongue moving
between its teeth, stilled but approaching,
coming, coming; at once huge
and far away, immensely tiny and close?

Nest

Dropped on the path from above this
minor masterpiece in feather, horse-hair,
moss and grass the size of my fist,
in its just-abandoned perfection

something of the kitchens of the disappeared
or dispossessed – breakfast a mossy fuzz,
coffee trembling on the table –

or the kitchen where we find ourselves
in this nest of hills and where I bring
this unit of beauty, this interior knot
just as the news on the radio drops

us onto the path of history, as if we've
woken into a field at dawn – naked, wet,
the steam still rising.

Twinned Sonnets

If I had one love, it was the one who sat
naked all night with me in the shower
after sex when I couldn't sleep, when I
hadn't slept for weeks, and made believe
we were in a rainforest on the other
side of the world and the water that fell
was a storm warmed by the equator,
the beat of the party beyond the wall
the death song of cicadas, the rain's
rapid chatter off the giant leaves
our talk, the breathing of the giant trees
our breath;

         caught once in a downpour
I crawled under a roof of hawthorn,
woven trunks a chair, window made of rain.
He came and sat with me, weightless yet warm –
a human warmth I hadn't known for years –
all I left behind come to join me here,
the whole my body makes of two halves
when it is alone, when I have walked far
enough into the woods to out-walk my death.
Rain shivered like glass held to the light
and I slipped out of mind or maybe I slept
when what came through me was another's breath.

        Selves collapse; time stands outside its box.
The exact next moment belongs to the fox

(Fox)

who walked through me the morning I was half-
asleep, half-awake, awake to another world,
a big dark dog fox blood-dark rising from the path
I'd stepped onto from the woods, trees a-blur
with rain, my material self forming from a slur
of slate grey dawn-light. A paw, claw-tipped,
peeled from my chest and the rest turned
a pirouette as if my skin was mist, as if my flesh
had shifted each atom – iron blooming
in my mouth, a lightning hit, hands tingling;
close-up its eyes were lit windows
where grandmother fox sat at her sewing,
        then, it was merely a fox that had stopped,
        startled by the human it had almost touched.

Counting the Pennies

How quickly the pennies tarnish
rubbed together in the penny barrel
like grain, not the silken rush
over the plunged-in hand but
the grit-feel of necessity, the stink
of it as it gilds the skin. Dad's pennies
on the shelf above the bed
pilfered for sweets, the gut-sing
of guilt, jangle, jangle,
his hand a fat-knuckled mammal
jumping in his trouser pocket.
Now though, enough to make
a scratch meal or the bus to town.
This broken-eyed penny pot is sour
as an unbleached bin,
your fingers as you count and bag
rusty with tannin, familiar as that
tang in the mouth when you have
run hard and far and for too long
or in the stream when you reach
between the rocks where the water
runs brown from bracken. Pennies,
pennies, for the eyes of the dead one –
don't look – he comes in the night
with his smell of cigarettes, ravelings
of smoke, the path unrolling
a sheet in the sun where you might
make passage; pennies for the dead
stacked like chimneys in a toy
mill town, rained-on black blocks.
Here: the portcullis; here: the head.

Swan Upping
after Stanley Spencer

Woman, what are you doing
with your mattress, that hauled
weight you're putting your back into,
and you, with the cushion

extending the pattern of your self?
Consider the black angle
of the punt the two men are discussing,
faces to the interior, how it cuts

across the step, which is a line
drawing the eye downriver.
Each figure is at work, even the watcher
on the bridge willing them to come,

come home, and the child, half lost
in foliage. Even the sky
would speak, troubled by tree-tops
and blown cloud. Three bound swans –

two waiting, one aloft
across the gap from boat to quay –
what are these – Angels? Bodies of light
held at the still centre.

The Frozen River

In this dream, the river is frozen,
it is not a river, perhaps, but a glacier
reaching to the horizon –
I mean this: that the river, or glacier, lifts
skyward and appears to disappear
or meet the air. Is this what matters?

Or that under my feet the frozen rifts
and ridges – the small hard waves
that are like skiffs of royal icing
on a Christmas cake – have started
to thaw so that I must pick my way
cautiously, judiciously, like a bear

(*a Polar Bear*) finding its paws
in the soggy melt where they should
have met the compact fluff and crisp
of snow on ice. But I digress. Somehow
people have been driving their cars
on the river leaving slushy tracks; this is

reassuring *and* disconcerting. The ice
can take my weight, I must only pick
carefully around the pools that are now
forming near the centre, where the river
threatens to collapse inwards towards
the dark eel of river freeing itself

beneath me in slow humps and lurches.
The river is in a faraway country where
the vendor of hot drinks and donuts parked
precariously at the river's edge politely bends
his tongue around my language and I've
never felt so at home as here, among

the cars and day-trippers and polar bears.
This is not an environmental poem, this
is nothing more than a dream poem; this may
not even be a poem. I ponder for a while
after waking whether I am missing
something. Suppose that however much

we ply the surface, worry the depths, pore
over the detail, there is always only ever
ahead of us the gravity-defying
sky-reach of the river/glacier, at once
suspended, at once inexorably moving
towards a horizon we will never touch.

Marsh Lily

Unable to find you in my father's book –
no flower as four-petalled, just-touched-
pink-tipped on white, clumped on a comb-
leaf stem – I've plumped for a made-up
name: Lily-of-the-Marsh or Wild-Grass-Rose
(maybe you're too common, common enough)
closing your almost see-through eye-lids,
dropping your heads as soon as picked.

But good enough to lie among and feel
for the wind when it comes headlong
through the grass, or the sun when clouds
shift. Good enough for the heart to shout
it's here and here and only here I feel,
after all these years, almost at home.

Praise Song

I.M. Jo Cox, MP

I write in praise of the taxi driver who takes me home with my shopping. He is a large man, moon-faced, soft-voiced, lambent against the car window. He leans over to let me in and there is that moment – a fissure of uncertainty. It's Christmas Eve, and he asks *are you ready for the celebration?* We talk of Eid, this year in December, the Winter Solstice, of ritual and bringing together. He offers me an image of his family – aunties, uncles, cousins, kids – seated on a big carpet, feasting for days, candles lit and scattered through the house throwing their light among the shadows; his father at home in exile. The day before, or that week, some week or other a bombing or street massacre. It crouches between us, a burnt thing smacking its lips, audible enough for him to raise it like a dais we both lift off from. I offer that photograph – you know the one – Trump and his cronies incumbent at The White House – a dozen ugly old white men, the only woman an aide half-seen adjusting the lamp behind them, and the space between us comes down to this: how those that govern work for power alone; we are the ordinary people of the earth, defined by what we have in common. At the gate he unloads my bags, shuts the boot, takes my fare, returns to the car and lifts a hand farewell, his every movement fluid, measured.

To a Dandelion

I will not, I will not pull you up, cock-
of-the-beds among the last of the tulips,
the narcissi like used up tea-bags,
the breaking blue of forget-me-nots.
A purple admiral with one torn wing
unfolds its proboscis and dips-dips-deep
into petals of dense bright birds' tongues,
butter yellow, singing your colour,

your field-full of sunflowers.

Who else does this – metamorphosis?
Just now a bullfinch sipping up your seed,
his blush halting my conversation.
Feather-head, fuzz-ball, blow-in-the-wind.
I see through shards of the cerebellum
as each hour scatters – a tender, ripped shining.

Moths

The trolley rolls under strip-lights
blazing into one unfolded wing. The nurse
holds my hand; I've asked her to see me through.

I give way to anesthetic on the second count.
I've made my pact. Wake to blinds caustic at the window.
Somehow it is morning, around me

at the foot of the bed, white coats and clipboards.
I have a whole new blood.
I feel it, flushing the old water of my bones.

No one asks what I saw.
The long black rectangle of nothing –
less than, more than that. If you filled a room with tar

and let it set then set it wheeling into space
until it comes to rest,
a solid mass hanging in the emptiness

you'd have it. You cannot fear it.
The hospital faces know: this is life; this is death.
Now the scar is a line pulled tight above my pubis.

It is past midnight, the temperature below zero
when frost makes stones of air,
craquelure of grass. I lean from the window

as owls sing cages for my breath.
More and more these days time folds around me
like a moth settling on glass.

Sestina for Rain

It comes in the night, like a mother, rain
stealing into our dreams, lulling us, *hush*
hush, a lullaby sung beyond the window,
curtains shut tight against streetlights
that now hiss and stutter, now flicker
yellow and out, yellow and out, a hand

passed over our eyes in a game. Take hands
in the street for the night dances, the rain
now a drummer drumming at our feet, *hush*
hush and together, the beat a window
to a collective dream. Lighter and light
we are turned and lifted – gold starts, flickers

against the earth's mirror. The dream flickers
and fails and morning steals the night, its hands
a lullaby on the sheets as the rain
flattens hayfields to a yellow hush
as *hush* go wind and rain at the window.
We'd almost forgive the rain if the light

were more forgiving and give up its light-
fingered steal on the morning. Night flickers,
yellow drifts of pollen on our hands
from a dream of hayfields. The street is rain-
rushed, rain-rocked, rain-sung, a lullaby, *hush*,
hush as rain dances open a window

into the earth. We stand at our windows,
a dream collective wishing the light
would shatter the steel-fall of rain, flickers
of yellow birds, a pair of gold hands.
Instead, the street is curtained with rain, rain
fills the fields, the lanes, as the drains go *hush*

hush, a lullaby. The street is all *hush*
hush with rain, a dream song at our windows
where we sit, collectively, and watch light
dim and stutter, dip, falter and flicker,
matches struck in the cups of our hands
against the night, against the wind, the rain

an incessant *hush*, *hush* at the window
where light flickers yellow and out, yellow
and out, our hands cups, the mothers of rain.

A Perfect Mirror

i. grasmere

First night here – spring snow flurries
    I sate a long time

        hail then rain, the lake
    slate-black, blown in cups and wavelets
        walked among the stones of the shore

the line of the mountains merging
        with the last branch of light from the north

    – water-light, scarlet-lit, peachy-gold –
        until my heart was easier

        and later

    over Silver How

        a clouded moon.

        *

I dream Coleridge's dream –
    black-haired woman, wild-faced, waking me
        into a moon-flooded room

    a very fine moonlight night, the moon shone

        is it you, Dorothy?

    dream a boat tethered at the water's edge
        wash away dirt
    to the under-gleam

like herrings in the water
a fish's silver scales

*

next morning on the path to Rydal
a heron fishing, a red squirrel

on the path a blind man
a woman begging
a little girl

now as then the lake
an image of stillness, clear as glass

in the hill's dips and crevices snow like lost silver

pebbles on the road glittered like silver
frostings among the stones of the wall

*

at sunset red lights behind Langdales
these hard times
these hard times
a terrible kind of threatening brightness

ii. migraine

you try and out-walk it, walk all day pushing on, pushing on
as if you can outstep the kamikaze men shimmying hand over
hand down the fine internal rope ladder of your skull, the
rain a percussive *te*-dum-*te*-dum on your neck, your scalp, and
like a fisherman slowly reeling in his catch hooked in the sole
of your foot, drawn through thigh, lumbar, the sparse cobbles
of your spine where the cord tightens; you cannot stop it, you
cannot; give in and allow the pain dominion of the vessels of
your brain, blood swollen with blood, a leech fattening, the
fat pulse in your crown where once the plates were soft and
open; if only they would un-fuse now and let the creature out,
the dirty brown water run

iii. loughrigg

I sit against the moss-legged hawthorn
      and watch the vale unfold
           a painted cloth
                 I lay upon the steep

      sun on the lake a blanket
           of crushed diamonds, the water
               spotted with sparkles

      cloud shadows moving across the hills, lilac scree
           thumbed in bruises
               until my heart dissolved

I think of your love for William and how
      it is like a mother's for a son –
           there's no word for it – illicit

perhaps, the other a mirror
           you fall into like falling
           into a pool, self into self
                dissolved

               *

from the Rays a huge rainbow pillar
           cuckoo call, bouncing far then near

    a glorious wild solitude under that
           lofty purple crag
               impossible, here now

      to be alone other than inwards
      and back to where you are
           a creature by its own self among them
           or a self

alone
among the May Day visitors

we fit together, frame within frame
or overlap
a lacquered box
vivid with birds, trees, flowers

fragrant when we lift the lid

time, sister, colour – *all colours*
all melting into each other

*

at Loughrigg Tarn I lie down
as the sun drops
the light
as I lay down the glittering silver line

above the surface
of the water

a dance of spirits that rose out of the water
a shoal of lights
rushing and dancing

something of strangeness – as if belonging
to a more splendid world

this world then, where we are, between two worlds

iv. garden, wood

I sit a long time in the arbor, sun
        softening everything, a fragment
          of lake
    a small pool
        glittering
   soft as velvet

  a thrush sings
        then as now
    in jaunty lines and jingles

and you are present for a moment
    planting peas in the garden
stopping to lift your head
    to the thrush that sings and sings
              a perpetual song

the garden a green bowl
    everything green
        overflowing with life

white walls of the cottage, surrounding fells
    at the centre

     the lake
     a perfect mirror

*

evening walk to Bainriggs, I lie a long time
   to hear the peaceful sounds of the earth

   Dorothy's song
               The voice of the air

     spots of rain, soft mist

looking up   beech leaves
     light green medallions

mossy beds of pillowed stone dark green
     the small white clover flower
        fairies buzzing
        under the earth

               *

walking back a diffuse light, and I think I see you
        in the lane as I turn

     a sky-like white brightness on the lake

       glimpses of lake like scattered stars

        stars like butterflies

    crows shapes   *of water passing*
         over the fields

      birds transparent as moths

v. dorothy's colour

Fire-like red among the tops of the mountains   we walk
all day,   climb Silver How   *scarlet beans, robin,*
butterfly   every view a   framed picture   *birches*
red-brown and glittering   drop into   Langdale   *yellow*
in the water as of cornfields,   *bright yellow*   *the pear*
trees, the ash   lie a while in   the hollows   *oak*
trees   putting forth little yellow knots of leaves   learning
this slow   *hills*   *orange;   clouds a saffron*
light   slow daydream and drift   *a tender soft*
green,   a vernal greenness upon the grass from
the   rains,   water perfectly unruffled all over like green
islands,   grass and trees a gem-like brightness,   greenness
a thousand times   more green   walking back,
the lake   *the lake a rich purple,   clouds in the*
sky soft purple   the still reflective blue   *blue*
of   blue-stone   sky fading into the pale blue   of
an eye   *streaked and   scattered over with islands of*
purple   in reverie   *my heart a vision*

vi. *flowers*

Late May and hawthorn in blossom
    white amidst the green

      wild columbines
the little star plant a star without a flower

    two hundred years ago now time
      a beautiful fold

distant birch trees   *large golden flowers*

      in the city square a field of flowers

the smell of them
    as we turn the corner

their heads upon stones
    as on pillows for weariness

    an hundred hearts
      stars of gold in the sun

bobbing and snapping at their ribbons

    all the beautiful colours

    the view from here
      golden, buttercup
        in the hayfields

        everywhere yellow

The Unicorn
after Rilke

It wasn't there, and yet we believed in it,
the milk-white beast, barleycorn twist of its
impossible horn, horn now proven
to be narwhal tusk; oh how we love proof.

It wove itself into the tapestry
of myth where we chained it in gold filigree;
let's say, yes, it is gold that enslaves it.
Its chaste self saves us if we imagine it.

In the garden where the pomegranate
evolves its own bloody secret
the creature that has never been
tentatively puts out one silver hoof,

shimmering and oblique as an antique
mirror into which we can no longer see.

Praise Song

I write in praise of summer, that idyll, waited for through the dark months: light growing from long nights to short, blossom scenting pavements, dandelion heads we blow the hours from, thirteen of them, white flowers of the hawthorn, the birds at dawn. Even when it rains all June we hold out, *it's coming, it's coming,* if only we are patient; the promise of summer our inheritance: hot days swimming in rivers, picnics in the fields, toast-smell of skin, sleepless in the heat, evenings translucent. Even when it rains all August, the hay ruined, land a soaked sponge, homes washed out, we bed down with our hope for next year, vitamin deficient. Here too I write of the Syrian woman who read and re-read the whole of Jane Austen through the long siege winter. It took me away, she said, as the bombs fell all night, to a perpetual summer, tea on lawns and pastel gowns as lights went out in the last hospital, dances and parlour games as they stripped the trees of leaves for dinner. Irony, humour. This is the art of survival. For when there is too much fear there is never enough summer.

Relics

i. Jane Austen's Writing Desk
(The British Library)

A plain wood box, hinged, opening
to a writing slope, compartments for pens,
a sheaf of paper, unmarked –
not your usual hoard of hidden scraps –
a handle each end, the whole to be locked,
carried – private, portable, practical –
a portmanteau primed with effects, half
in time half out of it; all these years
your spectacles artfully placed as if
you'd paused to answer the door,
the reader over your shoulder just missing
the shift of a dress along the floor.
But no, it is not like this, only posed
to suggest it behind the museum glass.

ii. Emily Brontë's Couch
(The Brontë Parsonage Museum, Haworth)

The couch they say you died on
is kept in the parlour for visitors,
souvenir hunters after your ghost
who fancy they hear tapping
when it's just a graveyard of crows

(or the wind wuthering over the hill)

hoping to catch a scent of you,
your pulmonary blood deep
in the weave or around a stud, an aura,
a blue cloud ringing a white sun.
What is known is the moment
you drew your eyes that last time

from the window. Oh, Emily –
you would have frightened me; you frighten me still.

iii. Dorothy Wordsworth's Cap
(Dove Cottage, Grasmere)

White, hand-sized, embroidered
with a plain edge to neaten a wild
dark head, sister to the blue-lensed
spectacles and ink-stained pen nibs,

the letter set, the silver teapot,
drafts upon drafts of poems.
All those thoughts capped
in a cotton-white milk-white caul

white and fluted as the wild white
foxglove, a rare find in the woods
among the purple; hardly a flower
more a purse to hoard its poison;

this cap holds enough pollen
to speed the heart towards its vision.

iv. Sylvia Plath's Dust
(*Yaddo Foundation, Saratoga Springs, NY*)

This came to me –

        a vial of dust

   from the attic

            where you wrote

     your poems

      of worms and

witchery,   hooked into voice

   like

difficult corsetry.   It's not much –

     sediment

        from the sea bed

              halfway

to oil,   halfway

      to pearl

    and when I

        shake it –

an Egyptian   gold baby

    that explodes

           on air

    when touched

Getting Lost

Clare did it, famously: once as a child
breaking his bounds, again as an adult,
losing one half of himself to the wild.
Unbound, bound. Finding the path by chance
and once in sight, home made strange.
One winter I found the edge of moor
and kept going across grass and heather
black with months of rain until nothing
I saw for miles made sense and a huge stone
wall presaged a fall of land. I feared the earth
would crumble beneath my feet, air cartwheel
my breath and stammered heartbeats
and the only thing to do was retreat,
in the corner of my eye the shapes of clouds.
How Churn Milk Joan became standing stone
at the boundary of three towns. How
stumbling across her long back at dusk
from the wrong side I thought myself lost,
facing south not north, and almost panicked
until a light glinted on at Foster Clough.

Woods in Snow

It is the fell hour of the year
and we should not have lingered,
but from the field the sky
opened its wings, its fire-brushed feathers.

Between the snow-weighted branches
the dark mists and glitters —
a far-flung galaxy brought near,
a spin of flakes bright as whispers,

and here — true, oh, be true to it —
this closeness of hands, eyes, hearts,
our stilled breath a skipped beat —
in the braided grass, the hind asleep.

Moon Walk

What are the Lunarians up to tonight?
You ask. There's the moon hanging mute

off the back of the hill. What sad mouths
it has, what limping eye, it keeps us awake

with its mooning. You know it is rock, gravity
holding it and us together and apart; a Soviet

poster shows a cosmonaut caught by a thumb
on the moon's hook. There's no God up there

it says, confirming what no one can confirm.
Before either of us was made, (your egg inside

my egg inside my mother) they sent Laika
for whom there was no return, only the marvel

of earth and the moon rising brighter, brighter
in the window of her craft. Whatever

they want us to believe, let's leave her there,
a moon goddess for the moon people

on their moonwalk, just like us out after hours,
we who know the Lunarian flag has stars.

Halfway Back

i.

The day's a beauty, sun on the minted
morning, fresh hint of air from the west.
The climb up Steeple track past the ox-eye
daisies, the piebald pony, the stone lintel
of the tumbled shack takes nothing from you,
nor the sheep path that veers left over rough
ground to the lip, the brow, then the crown
of the hill. Now's the time to sit and draw
in the valley's veined cupola, the next
county's border a raised vernacular
after all those flat vowels. You'd been advised
to cross an unmarked field and cut the walk
a whole arduous mile; razor wire folds
loosely around bog grass and a haze lifts
from the soft ground. But how to do this –
slip past the waymark when you see the farmer
on the road and no convergent distance?
Now you are the girl who folds into a note
and posts herself sky-wards like a white bird.
You keep right and pass a farm where dogs
are set to guard at intervals in separate yards.
Allow now a long down hill, a rough jog
slowing as the road rises to the crossroads,
and although south rolls to a village
you follow the map and set course north
for the plantation. It's midday, water's
low, your pack an extra kilo and lunch
must wait until you've placed a wall
between yourself and the curious cattle.

The walls are man-height, and you so small,
until the gate, tightly wrought barbed wire
and sheet iron layers over a nettled ditch.
She's back, the girl who can ride on air
and it's a snitch getting over this.
A cascade of tussocks on a sixty-degree
slope and you've made it to the creek
where you unlace your boots and sink
your feet into the cool singing waters,
eat at last on the heat of the bank.
Lie down with the land now; you're halfway back.

ii.

We could say that you never left, we could say
so much was lost – what was still to be
achieved, won, admired, loved; we could
imagine you halfway between here and there,
about to set off but, having forgotten something
essential, about to turn back. We could say
you are just out of ear shot, beyond calling
but not quite. We could say if only you'd
waited, not turned that corner, crossed that
crossing, breached that border, turned on
the gas. We could say a cloud's shape
suggests you, black arms of winter trees
shimmering in the rain, the mountain ash
in berry – the one we like to sit under –
where you hover, or a thought of you,
embodied enough. We could say that you
couldn't give a damn if we thought of you
or not. We could say that you are simply
checking out a new direction, distance,
dimension. We could say that you have
absconded for a while, entered a fugue state,
or that you have forgotten yourself like a passport
at the bottom of a drawer under a pile of socks;
the keys on the dresser everyone, at a certain age,
comes to forget. Perhaps we have mislaid
you and you are waiting until we remember
where you are. Perhaps you gave up the game
long ago. Perhaps that's you, sitting in silhouette
on top of the hill. What the dog looks askance
at as dusk falls in the lane. We could say
that you are halfway there, halfway back.

New Moon

This evening
>   the temperature drops
>   and the air is clear of rain.

>   The clip of moon
>   with its attendant hoop
>   like the bright-ringed bottom of a pan

catches an ember of winter sun
>   and you can

>   almost hear it – a sky-note rung
>   in the ear, at the finger-tips,

>   on the back of the tongue.

>   In the valley

>   the streetlight's cupped votives scatter
>   into the hills

>   and high above the town
>   the bank of cumulous

>   volcanoes.

>   One-by-one,
then in a rush – stars – a multitude
>   of eyes,

>   nocturnal creatures

>   lighting the dark wood.

Acknowledgments

Acknowledgments are due to the editors of the following magazines and on-line journals where some of these poems first appeared: *Stand, Strix, Poetry Review, The High Window, The Manchester Review, The John Clare Society Journal, Disclaimer.*

Thank you to Arts Council England for a time to write grant in 2011, which helped support the writing of this book, a Grants for the Arts grant for the project *Dorothy's Colour*, and The Wordsworth Trust, where the sequence, 'A Perfect Mirror' was written. A huge thank you to everyone at Pavilion Poetry, especially Deryn Rees-Jones who wove her magic once again and turned a bagpuss of a manuscript into a panther of a book. Lastly, but not least, to my son, Lugh, for his enduring patience, wisdom and love; this book is dedicated to you.

Notes

'A Perfect Mirror' is a phrase taken from Dorothy Wordsworth's *Grasmere Journals*, Oxford University Press Edition, 1982; the phrases in italics are also taken from the journal, and some have been rearranged. In 'Flowers', 'In the city square a field of flowers' refers to the flowers laid in Manchester City Centre after the Manchester Arena bombing in May 2017.

A version of 'A Perfect Mirror' was written and shown as part of *Dorothy's Colour*, a collaboration/exhibition with the visual artist Zoe Benbow, in partnership with The Wordsworth Trust and Lancaster University and funded by Arts Council England Grants for the Arts, Lancaster University Friends' Alumni Fund, and Lancaster University's Department of English and Creative Writing. A special thanks to Jeff Cowton at The Wordsworth Trust for the extensive support given to this project, The Peter Scott Gallery, Lancaster, and The Poetry Cafe, London.

In 'Warming', I quote from 'Snow Blitz', Sylvia Plath, *Johnny Panic and the Bible of Dreams* (Faber and Faber, 1977), page 132.

Halfway Back (i) was first published as 'An English Walk' *Poetry Review*, then in *Salt: The Best British Poetry 2012*; and shown as part of the touring exhibition 'Where We Begin to Look' 2013/14, curated by Deryn Rees-Jones in collaboration with Zoe Benbow and The Poetry Society.

'The Garden' was written after reading Nick Laird's poem of the same name in his collection *On Purpose* (Faber and Faber, 2007), and was first published in *The Manchester Review*.

'View of a Badger on the Heights Road', 'Marsh Lily', 'Twinned Sonnets', and 'To a Dandelion' were written in response to the sonnets of John Clare, and first published as part of a longer sequence in *The John Clare Society Journal*, summer 2014. Thank you to Niall and Nadia Munro for their advice on resolving 'Twinned Sonnets'.

'Nest' was written in response to the Brexit result on the 23rd June 2016, and first published in *Poem: International Journal*.

'Sixteen Acres' refers to Carr's Farm, Wadsworth, Hebden Bridge where this and many of these poems were written. My love and thanks to Gill Vile and her family for allowing me access to this beautiful place over the years; these sixteen acres have been more than home to me. I am also indebted to Deryn Rees-Jones for her image of Heptonstall Church, as seen from Wadsworth, as a wolf.

In 'Getting Lost', Churn Milk Joan is a standing stone that marks the boundary between three towns on Wadsworth Moor above Hebden Bridge. Many legends surround the stone, one being that 'Joan', lost one night on the moor in a snow blizzard, was turned to stone. The stone bears cup and ring marks and therefore may be Neolithic, but this is disputed; a fragment of more ancient stone rests beside it.

In 'Moonwalk', the 'Lunarians' are inhabitants of the moon in the *Final Fantasy* Nintendo game.

I am indebted to Claire Harman's *Biography of Charlotte Brontë* (Penguin Books, 2015) for the insights on Emily Brontë's death.